Philosophy for children

From child to children

Once upon a time!

The puppy that turned into a kitten!

Coloring story!

By: Bernardo Octaviano Pereira

This book belongs to:

____

I dedicate this work, firstly, to my parents who I love so much, to my teachers, to my dear aunts and to all my friends, may God bless you all infinitely!

Bernardo Octaviano Pereira

13/04/2024

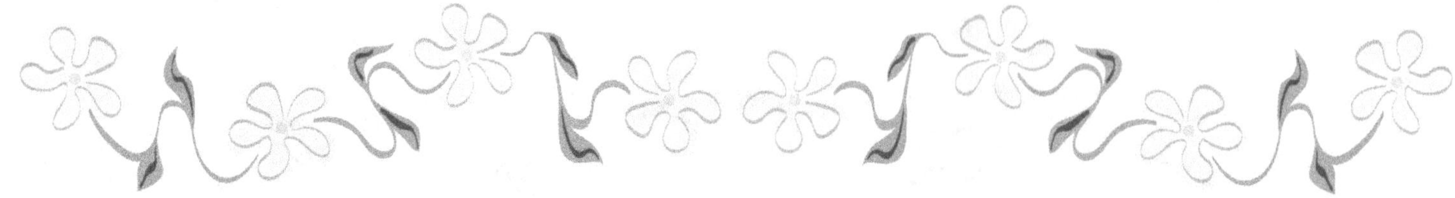

Once upon a time, in a place not far from here, a dog gave birth to several cute and fluffy puppies, and nearby a kitten also had several adorable and furry kittens;

And one day
the puppy
got away
from his
mommy and
got lost from
his family;

But as time went by, the very loving kitten found the puppy crying, and welcomed the puppy into her home,

and time passed, and the puppy was adopted and being raised like kittens, and his mother cat treated everyone the same;

Time passed and the puppy began to learn the ways of a kitten, such as jumping backwards, falling on its back and various other cat things that his little kitten brothers taught him;

One day they were playing in the street and the cart came by and arrested all the kittens and the puppy, taking them all prisoner and putting them all in cages;

One more of the kittens managed to open the cage and escape, releasing the other little animals and running to the patio,

where it was surrounded by a huge wall, where the kittens jumping on the wall and on the tree that was close to the wall climbed with great effort;

But the puppy wouldn't make it, it was too high for him, and the kittens screamed from the top of the wall; From above they encouraged the little dog to do the same, come little brother, jump on the tree and then on the wall, you will make it;

But the very scared little dog didn't believe he would make it, so when the guards ran with a net in their hands to catch him, he took a distance and jumped the biggest he had ever done;

He grabbed the tree and jumped onto the wall where his little brothers were waiting for him, they all jumped together to freedom.

The puppy, by believing in himself and his little brothers, overcame his difficulties and, over time, turned into a kitten. This story reminds us that, with determination and support,

We can overcome our fears and achieve our goals. Self-confidence and collaboration empower us. To transform ourselves into whatever we want to be. Believing in our potential is the first step towards overcoming.

The puppy believed in him and his little brothers, and overcame his difficulties by transforming into a kitten and managed to escape, we can transform into whatever we want, let's believe in our potential.

Let's believe in ourselves, and be whoever we want to be.

The end!